DROP BY DROP

The Buddha's Path to True Happiness

Ven. Bhikkhu Buddharakkhita

DROP BY DROP

The Buddha's Path to True Happiness

Bhikkhu Buddharakkhita

First published : May 2012

ISBN : 978-955-54359-0-1

Printed by : Creative Printers & Designers
3A, Bahirawakanda Road,
Kandy. Sri Lanka.
Tel: 081- 4940 668, 669
E-mail : creativekandy@hotmail.com
creativekandy@gmail.com

Published by : **Bhikkhu Buddharakkhita**
Uganda Buddhist Centre
Off – Entebbe Road, Bulega, Garuga, Entebbe,
P.O. Box 898, Entebbe,
UGANDA
EAST AFRICA
www.UgandaBuddhistCenter.org

DROP BY DROP

The Buddha's Path to True Happiness

Bhikkhu Buddharakkhita

ISBN : 978-955-54359-0-1

Price : US$ 3.95

CONTENTS

Dedication

The gift of the Dhamma exceeds all other gifts.

The flavor of the Dhamma exceeds all other flavors.

The delight in the Dhamma exceeds all other delights.

- The Buddha

This Dhamma book is humbly dedicated to my beloved Preceptor, the late Venerable Sayadaw U Silananda of Dhammananda Vihara, Half Moon Bay, California, U.S.A, who ordained me and encouraged me to learn and spread the Dhamma.

May he attain final liberation.

Acknowledgments

This book was inspired by many friends and students around the world. I would like to thank all of you:

To my mentor and teacher, Bhante Henepola Gunaratana, for his inspiration and guidance, and Sitagu Sayadaw, Beelin Sayadaw and Sayadaw U Osadha for their constant guidance and support.

To my mother, Felister Nampiima for giving birth to me and for her kind and loving support throughout my life.

My Ugandan friends and supporters, Princess Diana Teyeggala, Dr. Sekagya Yahaya, Tony Renart, Tom Muwanga Kaboggoza, Sandra Kisinde Kaboggoza, Frank Nelson Ntwasi, Dr. Juuko Ndawula, Dr. Mike Illamyo, Pablo Imani for their constant inspiration and friendship.

My benefactors, including the Bhavana Society, the Insight meditation Society, Spirit Rock Meditation Center, Buddhist Society of Victoria, Flowering Lotus Meditation Center, New York Insight Meditation Center, Sri Lanka International Buddhist Academy, World Buddhist Summit (Japan), Global Peace Initiative of Women, Mi Khin Khin Soe, Sisi Tan, Sarah Marks, Anh Mai Tu, John Haywood, Sarah Entine, Hon. Tofiri Kivumbi Malokweza, Hon. James Mulwana for their kind kind support.

To my student and friend, Ofosu Jones-Quartey, Dora King, Mona Wolven, Dolores Watson, Jiske Foppe, Kagendo Murungi and others for their inspiration and practice.

To my monastic companions, Ven. Dr. Khammai Dhammasami, Ven. Bhikkhu Nandisena, Ven. Bhikkhu Bodhi, Ven. Bhikkhu Anālayo, Ajahn Dhirapanyo, Ajahn Sona and many more for their generous support and friendship.

To Bhante Rahula, Walt Opie and Steve Sonne feld for their valuable suggestions.

To my International Dhamma friends, Kuku Gallman, Sveva Gallman, Dena Marriam, Joseph Goldstein, Jack Kornfield, Sharon Salzberg, Larry Yang, Gina Sharpe, Dr. Jo Nash, Konda Manson, Anushka Fernandapulle, Michele Benzamin-Miki, Prof. P.D. Premasiri, Dr. Sarath Chandrasekara, Prof. G.A. Somaratne and the teaching staff at Sri Lanka International Buddhist Academy for their kind inspiration and support. And thanks to my editor, Jonah Mix, for editing the book.

I am indebted to all of you.

Introduction

At the end of a meditation retreat, people come to me and ask a very important question: What do I do now? They think it is impossible to practice the Dhamma in the modern world. They want desperately to bring what they've been practicing back home with them, but they're afraid that the Buddha's teachings won't fit in a high-tech world of air conditioning, computers, cars, iPhones, and countless other modern trappings.

This fear is understandable. Most of us live a busy life full of constant melodrama. We have to earn a living, keep up our house, and deal with people both friendly and rude. We watch what we eat and drink. As compulsive shoppers, we spend most of our time in front of the TV or with a catalogue in hand, checking out the latest products for sale. In today's world, we deal with a million little things every minute of the day. It's no wonder that so many of us have a hard time believing that the Buddha's words can have anything to say about our lives today and an even harder time making time to find out!

Luckily, when we really examine ourselves, we'll see that the mind is the same for us now as it was for those who lived so many years ago during the Buddha's time. We may have new fancy distractions and addictions, but our struggle is no different from the struggle the Buddha himself went through, and the way to liberation from this struggle is no different either.

At the heart of this path towards freedom is meditation. Your gender or race, your age or religion, your monthly paycheck or anything you've done before this moment – none of it matters. Meditation is not about the content of our lives; it's about how we relate to our daily experiences, whatever they may be. Meditation is about waking up and seeing clearly how we're doing, what we're doing and why we're doing it. Meditation is a reality check.

Someone once asked the Buddha, "What do you and your disciples practice?" and he replied, "We sit, we walk, and we eat." The questioner continued, "But Sir, everyone sits, walks, and eats." The Buddha responded, "But when we sit, we know we are sitting. When we walk, we know we are walking. And when we eat, we know we are eating."

That's what meditation is. It's about breaking through our greed, hatred, and delusion, and just seeing the world with bare attention – seeing the silliness of our desires, the pointlessness of our aversion, and the bewilderment of our delusion. This is true happiness. This is inner peace. This is ultimate freedom. You don't need to go anywhere to find them. You just need to look deep into your mind and see that they're already there.

Despite the beautiful simplicity of this approach, we all still face the temptation to ignore the Buddha's teachings until we have more time. Some of us with family members may put it off until our children graduate from college. Some of us with demanding jobs will wait until we retire. Some attempt to deal with such a time crunch by reducing Buddhist meditation to a single technique or a single form - something to be practiced on the cushion only during sporadic retreats, or only once a day at a certain time between other tasks. Eventually, many simply give up the whole idea of meditation, or pick and choose certain techniques instead of embracing the whole of the Buddha's teachings. Before we know it, we're practicing in a shallow way, with little or no result.

But there is another way to approach the Dhamma. Instead of turning this life-changing meditation into a period of time we have to just "get through," or a distant goal we pursue and then lose in frustration, we can view our practice instead as an essential, yet gradual process of mental cultivation and purification - in the Pāli language, we call this bhāvanā. Bhāvanā is not a chore or a time commitment; bhāvanā is the way to a generous, loving, compassionate, steadied, wise, and joyful mind.

This booklet will show you the heart of Bhāvanā– the Noble Eightfold Path, the Buddha's ultimate guide for developing morality, concentration, and wisdom. If you diligently follow the steps laid out here, you can get up on your feet and starting walking the path towards liberation.

May all beings attain true happiness, inner peace and ultimate liberation.

The Noble Eightfold Path

The Wheel of Dhamma – another name for the Noble Eightfold Path, due to its eight branches being like spokes on a wheel – was first set spinning over 2,500 years ago, but its eight fundamental aspects still form the basis of our daily meditation practice. In this path, we find an indispensable framework for observing, reviewing, and improving the value of every single thing we do, from the time we wake up to the time we lie down in bed. The Noble Eightfold Path shows us how to achieve purity, compassion, and wisdom whether in our actions, words, or thoughts.

There is nothing in our meditation practice that cannot be found in one of the Wheel of Dhamma's eight spokes. Any skillful action finds its home inside this path, so long as it is done with the primary purpose of developing morality, generosity, loving–kindness, compassion, concentration, and wisdom. This is not a set of rules just for monks and nuns or a guidebook just for the most advanced among us; the Noble Eightfold Path can be practiced by anyone on this Earth who wishes to enrich their household lives through spiritual development.

The Buddha once said, "Think not lightly of evil, saying, '*It will not come to me.*' Drop by drop is the water pot filled. Likewise, the untrained person, the unwise man, gathering it little by little, fills himself with evil." Our daily lives are filled with thousands of actions, words, and most importantly, thoughts; together, these have a cumulative effect as we interact with others. If we ignore the Noble Eightfold Path, we inevitably behave in ways that cause suffering for ourselves as well as others. Such actions gather force with time, in turn defining our habits, our values, and our character. Not a single thought will go through our heads without leaving its mark, for better or for worse.

Luckily, the Buddha gave a second, more inspiring teaching: "Think not lightly of good, saying, '*It will not come to me.*' Drop by drop is the water pot filled. Likewise, the trained person, the wise man, gathering it little by little, fills himself with good." In our daily life, when we act or speak in skillful ways, inspired by the Eightfold Path, happiness for ourselves as well as others is bound to follow. Like the pot collecting water, these drops of righteous action will fill our mind in the end.

The key to living this happier and meaningful life - the key to filing our buckets with joy and skillful action - is the purification of the mind through the Noble Eightfold Path; this is right understanding, right thought, right speech, right action, right livelihood, right effort, right mindfulness, and right concentration. These skillful qualities of the heart and mind can be practiced daily in every aspect of life in order to bring about inner peace, true happiness, and ultimate freedom. As we start out on our journey, our first stop is right understanding, a mental state essential for parting the clouds of ignorance that block out the road before us.

I

Right Understanding

(Sammā Ditthi)

When one has right understanding, it means they have a correct view of the basic nature of the world within and around them. This includes the Buddha's teachings of the three marks of existence, the four Noble Truths, and finally the whole some and unwholesome states of mind as well as their roots.

The Three Marks

When the Buddha first sat down in meditation under the Bodhi tree where he gained his enlightenment, he soon realized three simple things about the universe. He saw with direct knowledge that all things are impermanent, without essential self, and ultimately unsatisfying. These three facts, which we now refer to as the three marks of existence, form the core of all Buddhist philosophy and practice. As Gotama realized these things, he became a Buddha, a perfect man free from all desire, devoted to bringing an end to ignorance and suffering in all living beings.

Unlike many spiritual traditions, this central truth is not based on divine revelation. No God descended to Earth and taught the Buddha these things. Instead, this life-altering insight came simply from his own profound wisdom, cultivated over many lifetimes of seeking. And just as he came to know the truth so many years ago, so can we understand the very same truths that lie inside of us, clouded by ignorance. In fact, the very core of our meditation practice is exactly this – realizing that freedom from suffering is in our grasp, right here and right now.

Impermanence (Anicca)

Anicca, or impermanence, is the first characteristic shared by all things. The Buddha taught us that everything is in constant flux, never staying the same from one moment to the next. Nothing in the universe can escape this unending cycle of change. Even the things that look and seem immovable and eternal are in reality relentlessly evolving moment by moment, disguised by the imperceptible nature of the transformation. On a long enough time scale, even the largest mountains will be ground into dust; please think about how much faster the things we love will break down and wither away.

Our physical bodies are a perfect example. They appear to be solid, steady, always fundamentally the same. But in reality, our bodies are changing all the time. Old cells are dying and new cells are taking their place. It only takes seven years for all cells to die and be supplanted; you may peek at a photo from the past and think you haven't changed much in that time, but in fact, nothing about you is the same at all!

The same impermanence can be seen in our thoughts and feelings as well. When we feel anger, many of us cannot see ever being happy again – yet ten minutes later, we're smiling and laughing, completely different people. Thoughts come into existence and vanish the next instant. We make decisions with life-changing consequences, all for a feeling that will be gone in the blink of an eye! If only we could realize the true nature of impermanence. The most massive stars will die out, as will the most fleeting thoughts. It is the basic essence of all things to arise and fade. Nothing can escape this cycle - everything is permanently impermanent!

Please remember, this does not mean that we disregard the things we own or the people we love. We simply make an effort to understand that although we have them to cherish and enjoy now, we will not always. We must act with compassion and kindness, loving without clinging. In this way, we free ourselves from possessiveness and jealousy while enjoying things fully in the moment we have them. Taking time to slow down and pay attention to the signs of impermanence can help us let go of attachment and make the most of what we have.

Dissatisfaction (dukkha)

Literally, the Pāli word *dukkha* just means what is difficult to bear; it has a connotation of suffering, disharmony, or dissatisfaction. It is very difficult to find an English word that does justice to the true meaning of dukkha; in fact, it's a cause of suffering to even try! Most think that it is better not to translate the word at all.

Dukkha is the central teaching of the Buddha, who saw all existence as riddled with suffering. This is not to say that we don't experience happiness; however, these moments are fleeting, an iceberg's tip that shows over an icy ocean of dissatisfaction. If we take the time to mindfully examine ourselves, we can see that neither sensual pleasure nor physical wealth ultimately satisfy us. This isn't a shocking revelation – spiritual teacher after spiritual teacher has said the same. What sets the Buddha apart is his method for dealing with what seems like an unfixable problem.

The Buddha taught us to pay close attention to our suffering and dissatisfaction so that we may understand them fully. This seems silly at first; most of us think that we know very well when we suffer and when we don't. And indeed, it is very easy to know the gross suffering that comes from injury, illness, and heartbreak. But this is only a small segment of our whole encounter with dissatisfaction. If we examine the whole of our experiences mindfully, we can see that neutral or even positive experiences are tinged with sorrow. We delight in our beauty, but deep down we know that it will not last. We may buy a brand new sports car, but somewhere in our mind a voice says, "It could have been fancier." We attend parties and convince ourselves that we are enjoying the night, but anxiety, fear, and self-consciousness are only inches below the surface.

The Buddha saw this and realized that no impermanent thing could ever bring lasting happiness if it is guaranteed to fade away in front of our eyes. So long as all existence is enveloped by this constant change, suffering cannot be far behind. Just as a grey hair points to our aging, this impermanence points to our suffering. We can trace the entirety of our dissatisfaction and sorrow to our attempts to continually grasp that which we crave – a perfect body, a fat paycheck, a happy spouse, or anything else that can never last. If we treat the temporary as eternal, we will only find suffering.

Selflessness (Anattā)

Anattā is often the hardest mark of existence for people to understand. Simply put, it means that there is no permanent core or essence inside anything which can be called a self or a soul. Instead, what we perceive to be the self is made up of what the Buddha called the five aggregates of clinging: body, feelings, perceptions, mental formations and consciousness. It is best to imagine the self as a knot made by tying five strings together; we can see the knot, but we know that it does not really exist apart from the five strings that make it up. "Knot" is just a word we have to describe the coming together of many different strings. In the same way, what we imagine to be the self is really just the intersection of many different processes, all of which are impermanent. Just like you couldn't lay out the ingredients of a cake before baking, point to one, and say, "That is the essence of the cake," neither can we take a look at the various thoughts, feelings, emotions, and physical experiences that make up the whole of our being and say, "This is the essence of me."

One easy way to see selflessness is to examine our minds closely and see how little control we truly have over what arises. If there were a central soul or guiding essence, we would be able to control ourselves completely – yet we all know this is not the case. Because who we consider to be "us" is nothing more than the intersection of hundreds of varied thoughts, emotions, desires, and concepts, complete control is out of the question.

Meditation is a great tool to help us understand the selfless nature of the mind. When we slow down or sit and examine the mind, we are able to see various thoughts arise and cease together. Without mindfulness, the mind is like a muddy bowl of water. It may look uniform and unvarying, but when you give it time to be still, you can begin to see the many parts that make it up – the dirt, the water, the reflecting light, the pebbles, and so on. In the same way, we can realize during meditation that while our minds may seem to be ruled by consistent self, in reality we are simply a swirling mixture of innumerable thoughts, sensations, emotions, and concepts.

What's the Point?

Once, a man came to the Buddha and simply said, "I want happiness." The Buddha replied, "First, remove the 'I.' That's ego. Then, remove 'want.' That's desire." The Buddha smiled. "Now, you are left with only 'happiness.'"

Understanding these three marks of existence is the first step towards realizing for yourself the path to freedom from suffering. Although this ultimate liberation is our final goal, even a simple understanding of the Buddha's teachings on impermanence, dukkha, and selflessness can immediately bring about happiness, peace, compassion, generosity, joy, and contentedness. Through insight into impermanence, we can abandon our clinging and develop generosity; through insight into suffering, we can overcome ill-will and cultivate deep compassion and through insight into selflessness, we can discard delusion and develop great wisdom. As we begin to see these three marks of existence in our daily lives, we prepare ourselves to tackle the next teaching of the Buddha, the Four Noble Truths.

The Four Noble Truths

A right understanding of the three marks of existence leads directly to a right understanding (or right view) of the four Noble Truths, at least on a conceptual level. This understanding is incredibly important; our ability to practice meditation hinges on the way we understand the truth of our *dukkha*. According to the venerable American monk Bhikkhu Bodhi, "Right view is the forerunner of the entire path, the guide for other factors."[i] Right understanding is simply the act of understanding the Four Noble Truths. These four elemental statements about our existence were rediscovered and developed by the Buddha 2,500 years ago, but they are still completely true for us today.

The Four Noble Truths are dissatisfaction, the origin of dissatisfaction, the cessation of dissatisfaction, and the path that leads to the end of dissatisfaction. The Buddha acknowledged that suffering is part of human existence, and his teachings on the four Noble Truths of suffering are geared toward freeing all humans from that suffering by illuminating the root cause.

The First Noble Truth

The Saccavibhangasutta of the Majjhimanikāya[ii] provides an overview of the Noble Truths beginning with the first Noble Truth, the Noble Truth of Suffering: *birth, aging, sickness, death, sorrow is suffering. Lamentation, physical pain, mental displeasure, despair is suffering. Association with the hurtful, whether they are our enemies, unfriendly co-workers and bosses, strangers, and abusers is suffering. Separation from the beloved ones, whether they are our spouses, parents, relatives or friends, is suffering. Not getting what one desires is suffering. In short, clinging to the five aggregates of clinging is dissatisfaction.* This is essentially a restatement of the second mark of existence, namely that suffering is an undeniable fact of life here on Earth.

The Second Noble Truth

The Second Noble Truth is the truth of the cause of suffering. The Buddha said that the cause of suffering is craving for sensual desires, craving for being and craving for non-being. Craving and clinging is the principal cause of dissatisfaction in our personal lives, but you don't even have to look far into any aspect of our greater society to see the strife it causes there as well. In the Madhupindikasutta[iii], the Buddha traces the cause of all war and conflict to craving and selfish desires. Due to our unskillful desires, the Buddha said, kings fight with queens, husbands fight with wives, and brothers fight with sisters. Our impulse to chase after what we desire and run away from what we don't leads us into terrible suffering. We grow up being told that we are happiest when we are surrounded by material wealth and pleasure, but no one on this planet can argue that attachment to those things brings more sorrow than joy. The more we hoard around us, the more time we spend trying to satisfy desires we cannot possibly quench, the more we lose track of the things we truly care about: peace, happiness, and freedom from suffering. One day, I saw a passing car with a bumper sticker that said *Less stuff, more fun!* That's the Second Noble Truth – we only suffer because desires for things that end up hurting us. The less we desire, the more joyful we are!

The Third Noble Truth

The Third Noble Truth is the truth of the cessation of suffering and the realization of Nibbāna, the ultimate happiness. The Third Noble Truth tells us that although we suffer now, we don't have to forever. Peace, joy, and freedom from suffering can come to us when all craving is abandoned. As we gradually leave behind greed, hatred, and delusion, the roots of unhappiness, then we will no longer suffer from the effects of such unwholesome mind states. Such are the fringe benefits of our meditation practice. However, when taken further, meditation can also lead us to the end of cycle of birth and death, the highest goal which we call Nibbāna. Though Nibbāna is the indescribably joy of freedom, the Buddha described it as peace and mental health.

Due to lack of understanding, many people speculate about the nature of Nibbāna endlessly. By the time they finish running in philosophical circles, they have a hard time believing that such a final destination is even possible because they can't explain it in easy terms. But for those on this Earth still stuck in the cycle of birth and death, still clouded with ignorance, and still struggling with craving and desire, there is no way to fully comprehend the nature of Nibbāna. For those who have trouble understanding this, the Buddhist story of the Turtle and the Fish shows clearly how futile it is to try and describe something so outside our own ordinary experience.

> *There was once a turtle that lived in a lake with a group of fish. One day the turtle went for a walk on dry land and did not return for a few weeks.*
>
> *When he finally arrived home, he met some of the fish who had been missing him. The fish asked him, "Mister Turtle, how are you? We have not seen you for a few weeks. Where have you been?"*
>
> *The turtle said, "I was up on the land. I have been spending some time there lately."*

The fish were a little puzzled and they asked, "Up on dry land? What are you talking about? What is this dry land? Is it wet?"

The turtle replied, "No, it is not."
"Is it cool and refreshing?" the fish asked.
The turtle objected, "No it is not."
The fish continued to ask, "Does it have waves and ripples?"

"No, it does not have waves and ripples," the turtle replied. The fish asked, "Can you swim in it?"

The turtle emphatically replied, "No, not at all!"

The oldest fish scoffed and said, "It is not wet, it is not cool, there are no waves, you can't swim in it. This dry land of yours must be completely non-existent! It is nothing but imagination, nothing real at all."

The turtle laughed and said, "Well, maybe so." He turned and left the fish to walk on dry land once more."[iv]

Like the fish, we cannot possibly understand something as foreign to us as Nibbāna. However, if we approach with a humble mind free of arrogance, and wrong view, we can learn to trust those who have reached the dry land of freedom from suffering and learn to follow in their path.

The Fourth Noble Truth

The Fourth Noble Truth is the way to the cessation of suffering. This way to travel from the misery of greed, hatred, and delusion into the perfect freedom of non-attachmentis this very Noble Eightfold Path: right thought, right speech, right action, right livelihood, right effort, right mindfulness and right concentration.

The wholesome states, the unwholesome states, and their roots

Before we begin the practice of meditation, it is very important to have a clear understanding of what we're looking for. We must understand not only the difference between unwholesome and wholesome behaviors, but also their roots in our daily lives. In the Sammāditthisutta of the Majjhimanikāya, the Buddha states that "...a noble disciple understands what is unwholesome, what is the root of unwholesomeness, what is wholesome, what is the root of wholesomeness..."[v] If we are to transform our minds – the bhāvanā we discussed earlier – then we must first realize what causes us to develop destructive mind states. Fortunately, the Buddha spelled out ten unwholesome courses of action, namely: killing living beings; taking what is not given; sexual misconduct; false speech; malicious speech; harsh speech; gossip; covetousness; ill-will; and wrong view. He also made it clear that the roots of these unskillful behaviors, whether they manifest in action, speech or thought, are greed, hated and delusion. These three unwholesome states are the basis for all suffering, and they must be eliminated before peace, joy, and freedom can be achieved.

To cover the wholesome side of our minds, the Buddha simply negated the ten unwholesome actions and their roots by advocating: abstaining from killing living beings; abstaining from taking what is not given; abstaining from sexual misconduct; abstaining from false speech; abstaining from malicious speech; abstaining from harsh speech; abstaining from gossip; abstaining from covetousness; abstaining from ill-will and abstaining from wrong view. Similarly, the roots of these skillful behaviors, whether they manifest in action, speech or thought, are non-greed (generosity), non-hated (loving-kindness) and non-delusion (wisdom). These three wholesome states are the basis of all joy, and they must be cultivated before peace, joy, and freedom can be achieved. Once we can identify these positive and negative mind states, we can easily avoid any situation that leads to suffering while following that path that leads to happiness.

Once we have the above three kinds of right understanding, we can cultivate wholesome thought as the path continues to unfold.

II

Right Thought
(Sammā Sañkappa)

To have right thought is to develop thoughts of non-greed (generosity); thoughts of non-hatred (loving-kindness) and thoughts of non-cruelty (compassion). The Buddha illustrated the benefits of such behavior in the very first two verses of the Dhammapada. The first verse states, "Mind precedes all mental states. Mind is the chief; they are all mind-wrought. If with an impure mind a person speaks or acts, suffering will follow him like the cartwheel follows the foot of the ox."[vi]

In the above simile, although there is a gap between the wheel of the cart and the foot of the ox, one will still eventually pass where the other has gone. In the same way, we will inevitably have suffering strike us if we follow the path of an impure mind. This is due to our tendency to speak or act in ways that are greedy, hateful, cruel, or deluded when thoughts of greed, hatred, cruelty, and delusion arise unchecked by mindfulness. We tend to yield to unwholesome impulses and forget their repercussions. Sometimes, even if we do anticipate the result of our actions, we still try to get away with our unwholesome behavior by blaming others and abusing their trust. We might take advantage of the legal system with a fancy lawyer or make a million other fruitless attempts to not own up to what we've done. We think, "Well, I would have been punished if I had really done anything wrong," or we try and pretend that those we've hurt had it coming to them. But no amount of rationalizing will help, and sooner or later suffering catches up. Even if we win the case or escape consequence at work, in the final analysis, we end up with nothing but regret, shame, and sorrow.

The second verse of Dhammapada states, "Mind precedes all mental states. Mind is the chief; they are all mind-wrought. If with a pure mind a person speaks or acts, suffering will follow him like his never-departing shadow."[vii] Interestingly, in the above simile, there is no distance between our shadow and the wholesome person. This shows clearly the immediate joy we feel when we speak or act with a pure state of mind. And while the ox cart was burdensome and heavy, the shadow is light and free. You've never felt weighed down by your shadow, have you? Likewise, there is buoyant lightness in the joy and happiness brought on by our good deeds.

But what does it mean to have these thoughts of non-greed, non-hate, and non-delusion? To have thoughts of non-greed simply means to nurture mind states that support giving and sharing our possessions, both material and immaterial, with others. Generosity can be the giving of material goods or the giving of service; to offer food, clothes, or anything that another person may find helpful is to have right thought. We can even practice giving away immaterial things such as our time, ideas, kind words or just a smile. A smile is a natural expression of a relaxed body and mind; generously donating it for another person is a beautiful act of non-greed.

Sadly, immaterial things can often be the hardest to give away. Many people can donate a multitude of possessions but never a minute of their time. We are often quite attached to our free time because it is so much closer to our ego. If you find it difficult to donate your time to others, please do try and aid or simply comfort those in need when you have a spare moment. There is a Chinese proverb, "If you want to be happy in your life, help others." It is a great opportunity for cultivating right thought to be able to share your time with others. Please consider some volunteer work for non-profit organizations. Practice sharing your accomplishments with others and rejoice in others' success. These practices not only help others but also enrich you spiritually as well. Giving will help you to weaken or overcome self-centered desires and attachments.

The other part of giving practice is about giving others an opportunity to give. Therefore, we should learn to gracefully accept offering from others. Due to arrogance, conceit, and pride, most people do not want to accept small gifts from others. Thus, they deny others the opportunity to practice generosity. We should be good receivers as well as givers!

With generosity, you can achieve far greater happiness here and now as well as in the future. Paradoxically, when you give, you get!

Yet, among all these wonderful expressions of generosity, there is a higher form of giving. By maintaining the five precepts, we can offer the great gift of fearlessness, security and freedom. According to the Buddha, the highest form of giving is the giving of the Sublime Truth (Dhamma). Offering the truth of the Buddha's teaching to anyone in pain is a beautiful expression of generosity. But don't worry if you can't become a monk; as Bhante Gunaratana said, "Though becoming a monk or nun is indeed one way of practicing generosity, most people can let go in the midst of busy, family-centered lives."[viii] We don't need to do anything incredible. Out of loving-kindness, we can give away some of our shoes or clothes to others in need. This is enough to bring great benefit to us spiritually. When we let go unnecessary things, even our unskillful mind states, we can experience greater happiness and freedom of both the heart and mind.

Another aspect of non-greed is letting go of the things that we don't need, instead of clinging to them. First, we should let go our unskillful physical and verbal behaviors. Afterwards, an even higher form of renunciation involves letting go of the negative emotions in the mind that keep us from developing peace, happiness and concentration. If you can't reach a state of proper concentration during meditation, please examine yourself and see if, at some level or another, you're not letting go of something that is distracting you. Most people want to concentrate, but they do not want to let go of negative thoughts and feelings. But we can't have our cake and eat it too! You'll be so much happier if you let those negative mind states slip away in favor of peaceful concentration.

Finally, the highest form of renunciation is letting go of the subtlest defilements: greed, hatred and delusion. We should begin with examining carefully the danger inherent in the blind pursuit of sensual desires. Even a small amount of introspection would show us that such craving is destructive and encourage us to seek renunciation. Remember, this letting go is not blind avoidance or repression; rather, it is a natural outcome of our deep understanding that while sensual pleasures may bring a short burst of excitement, they can never bring real permanent happiness. Because the objects of our desire are always changing, we must continually chase after them if we are to maintain the same level of excitement – a meal ends, so we eat another and another until we're sick. Our fancy car breaks down, so we spend more and more money to keep it shiny and new when we know deep down that we can't keep it from falling apart eventually. This craving ends up bringing even more suffering than happiness. However, the highest form of renunciation results in true happiness; in fact, the amount of negative mind states you dispel is directly proportional to your happiness!

Just like generosity, our daily life is filled with plenty of opportunities to practice loving-kindness, especially when the mind is inclined towards other wholesome thoughts. We can react to difficult situations with anger and hate, but this will only bring misery upon ourselves. Instead, please try and respond with understanding and compassion. Remember the bright spots and wonderful qualities in ourselves and in others, rather than focusing only on the weakness and faults. Many people do hundreds of great things, but once they do one single wrong thing, we blow up! They might forget to take out the trash or say one mean word, and without mindfulness, we can instantly feel anger and hate. This is a perfect time to practice loving-kindness. With it, we can learn to forgive others and give them another chance. We can always forgive others. Loving-kindness, or mettā, practice is by far the easiest to put into use in our daily life. Try to foster loving-kindness while driving, waiting in the line at the mall, or having simple conversations.

It is quite easy to practice loving-kindness at home with our family members. For instance, we can schedule some of our meditation sessions around a communal activity such as dinner time. Once the whole family has gathered, we can begin to radiate loving-kindness, beginning with ourselves. Repeating the following phrases in your own language might be helpful. We always begin with ourselves, and then we move gradually to our parents, relatives, teachers, friends, unfriendly people, indifferent people, and then finally all beings. Some of the recommended phrases are given below; you can use any phrases that resonate with you.

- May I be safe and secure (freedom from inner and outer harm)
- May I be happy (mental happiness)
- May I be healthy (bodily happiness)
- May I live at ease and in peace (may my relationships with others not be contentious)

After you say, “May I be safe and secure” or “May I be healthy,” say “May my parents and relatives be safe and secure” or “May my parents and relatives be healthy” before moving on to your friends, acquaintances, enemies, and finally to every being. It is delightful to start dinner having just wished “May all beings live at ease and in peace.”

When I think of mettā meditation, I am reminded of my woodstove during the cold winters in West Virginia. One winter, I was provided with wood that was half soaked and difficult to ignite. I tried many different ways to keep myself warm but it was always a challenge to get the fire going! Finally, I decided to light the stove by first putting in a small scrap of paper that would catch fire easily. Then I would place kindling over that, followed by a big hunk of dry wood; only after the fire started going strong, could I put the wet wood. This is how mettā works: the small paper is the loving-kindness we send to ourselves, the small kindling represents mettā to a friendly person and a neutral person, and the big wood represents all beings. Finally, the wet wood stands for the unfriendly person; while it was difficult at first to set it alight, I could do so with the support of the earlier dry wood. In the same way, by radiating loving-kindness out towards yourself, your friends, and neutral people first, it becomes possible to have the same feelings toward those who are unfriendly.

Mettā doesn't have to end when you get up from meditation. We can practice all these right thoughts while driving. Practice generosity by yielding to other drivers. Practice loving-kindness towards all beings in a traffic jam by not reacting with anger towards your fellow drivers. Practice patience at stop lights. And when someone drives recklessly and cuts us off, we practice compassion rather than getting angry. The Buddha said that when the mind is free from unskillful states of mind, it becomes gladdened, joyful, tranquil, and focused. With continuous practice of loving-kindness, we can experience a greater degree of freedom in the heart and mind.

Patience

Patience (Khanti in Pāli) is a wise, understanding acceptance that allows us to endure both the desirable and undesirable. It is the coming together of tolerance, endurance, and forgiveness. Neither rushing nor postponing, but confidently persisting. Patience allows us to enter any situation with gentle kindness and strength. Patience is really just mindfulness Practiced over and over! Concepts and habits lead us to anger while mindfulness allows us to see things as they really are and accept our circumstances with grace and serenity. Whether we are dealing with a pain in our legs or an unpleasant coworker, patience is the key to responding in a healthy way to the problems we face, both in the world and in ourselves.

During our daily activities, we should learn to be patient. In this harried, lightning-fast society, we never pace ourselves. We rush back and forth, never resting or taking a breath. Break this habit! Practice pausing before you respond to situations. When a phone rings, don't throw yourself across the room to answer it; settle in and compose yourself during the first few rings. When someone says something hurtful, don't snap back; take a few breaths to patiently examine how you feel.

It is a great idea to do nothing for one minute every hour. Relax the body and mind. Freeze any activity that is not absolutely crucial for just a moment and take a quick snapshot of where you are. Breathe in and breathe out. Let go of the past and the future. Say to yourself, "Breathing in, may I be well, happy, and peaceful." After a moment, say again, "Breathing out, may all beings be well, happy, and peaceful." These little flashes of mindfulness, awareness and loving kindness can fill your day with joy. Remember M&Ms, those little sugar-coated chocolate candies so many of us love to snack on? Think of these as Buddhist M&Ms – little 'mini meditations' that you can take any time for a quick treat.

Regularly pausing this way will help to slow down the neurotic push into the future we can so easily get caught up in, and help us release the stress that builds up throughout the day. With patience and slow, deliberate, mindful actions, we can reach home refreshed, even energized enough to do another round of meditation! Meditation before bed can help with deeper, more rejuvenating sleep. And with better sleep, we can wake up fresh and ready to set out on a new day. This makes us even more likely to keep a morning meditation practice! This chain reaction may seem like an oversimplification, but the benefits of just a few mindful minutes a day cannot be overstated. There's a bumper sticker I've seen that says it best: "A mindful thought a day keeps the suffering away."

Thoughts of Compassion

Thoughts of compassion involve opening our hearts and minds to all beings that are suffering in the world and cultivating awareness towards the interconnectedness of all beings. Through compassion meditation, one can be kinder towards all beings as well as oneself. Compassion is empathizing with other peoples' dissatisfaction. It arises when we mindfully notice the pain and helplessness in those overwhelmed by suffering. Some people have tendencies of turning a blind eye and plugging their ears when they see people who are dissatisfied; they do not see their own suffering, much less the suffering of others. They fail to accept or acknowledge the truth, instead living in denial.

But there is a better way to be found through the practice of compassion! Compassion is looking at life not with greed, but generosity; not with hatred, but loving-friendliness; with understanding, not delusion; and with courage, not fear. Compassion is letting go, not holding on: we have to stop chasing the things that cause us suffering. If we let go of our selfish desire, we will be practicing great compassion for both ourselves and others. As desire loses its grip on us, we begin to respond, not react, to situations. We can respond to suffering with non-hatred and with gentleness, instead of reacting blindly with aversion and anger.

Compassion means the courage to face suffering; it is not coupled with fear. Real compassion does not shrink away, but instead takes a challenge head-on. If we lack mindfulness, we can be overwhelmed by grief or sadness and find ourselves paralyzed. This behavior is dangerous; while it may seem like a natural result of compassion, in reality it prevents us from exercising true effort to improve the situation. Just as aversion and apathy stifle compassion, so to can unmindful empathy!

As we slowly learn to let go of our attachments and love others with bravery and honesty, compassion will lead us to understand life in its fundamental nature; we will no longer need to break our experiences up into "good" and "bad" groups, but instead face both our joyful moments and our great suffering with an open heart.

Most people simply become confused when faced with suffering, unable to accept the difficult parts that we tend to shut into the corner and ignore. Sickness, aging, death, and pain are all unfortunate but unavoidable parts of living in this world, and to ignore them leaves us unable to fully love and embrace others as well as ourselves. If we don't break out of a lifestyle where we run from the things we label “bad” and chase the things we label “good,” compassion will always struggle to arise. We will continue to suffer as our unhealthy, idealized worldview fights against the realities of life.

When practicing compassion, we begin with a person who is experiencing dissatisfaction or with a person in pain, and then follow the same order as we did with Mettā meditation: Ourselves, neutral persons, unfriendly persons, and finally all beings.

- “May I be free from inner and outer harm.”
- “May I be free from physical and mental dissatisfaction.”
- “May I be free from dissatisfaction and its causes.”
- “May I be free from craving or attachments... hate or anger... delusion or confusion... fear or sadness.”
- “May I be free from pain.”

We should continue to radiate the thoughts of compassion through all the categories, ending with all living beings. Through the practice of gratitude, generosity and contentment, we can find abundance for ourselves. This practice of loving-kindness and compassion leads to healthier inter-personal relationships with friends, children, co-workers, family, and all the other beings you may meet in your life. By cultivating such wonderful mind states, you can bring joy and happiness to yourself as well as others.

Equanimity

Equanimity (upekkhā in Pāli) is all about seeing things with an unprejudiced, impartial mind. To have a balanced mind is to see all people and all situations equally, not jumping to condemn or judge the things that we don't like. Life is a series of ups and downs; sometimes we find pain and sometimes we find pleasure. A mind that has developed equanimity can see all these peaks and valleys objectively without clinging or rejecting anything. A balanced mind simply sees things mindfully and lets them pass.

By cultivating equanimity, we can deal with difficult situations anywhere. We should maintain objectivity in daily life when faced both with agreeable and disagreeable circumstances, especially when it comes to what are called the eight worldly winds: pleasure and pain, gain and loss, praise and blame, honor and dishonor. These winds, like the winds we feel blowing every time we step outside, cannot be sped up or held back; but rather than let them blow us to and fro, we can simply stand tall with a stable mind.

We cannot keep pain away and we cannot hold on to pleasure. However, we do have two choices: we can run back and forth, scrambling to hold down our favorite things while we waste our time , energy and money in the quest to keep anything we dislike at bay, or we can simply be mindful of both great pain and great pleasure. The first response leaves us exhausted, bitter, numb, and shallow. This cycle of clinging to what we love and running from what we hate is a life lived on eggshells, where joy is smothered and squeezed lifeless while pain haunts us like a ghost. A life lived with equanimity, however, allows us to come to peace with our pain while reaching deeply into the true beauty of our experience. Equanimity is not whitewashing our lives, either suppressing or repressing emotion; quite the opposite, a balanced mind is one that penetrates deep below the surface of greed, hate, and confusion to find the pure reality we so rarely glimpse.

The two mental states of right understanding and right thought fall under wisdom. This wisdom becomes the basis and support for the ethical conduct in the next steps. It means that our speech, actions and livelihood will be based and supported by profound wisdom, generosity, boundless loving-kindness and deep compassion.

III
Right Speech
(Sammā Vācā)

Harmoniously living with oneself and others requires the practice of right or skillful speech, mainly through the development of gentle, loving communication skills. We say what is truthful with a right attitude of loving-kindness, making sure to speak at the right time and place. If we engage others in this way, we can avoid the four kinds of unwholesome speech: false speech, malicious speech, harsh speech, and useless speech.

Truthfulness is not merely the absence of false speech, but also the presence of honesty and openness. It means not pretending to be what you are not or refusing to accept things as they really are. We must be honest if we are to face the more difficulty aspects of our life. To do otherwise is to live in self-denial. And like all delusion, dishonesty will lead us down a path of suffering if we do not try to cultivate speech that is truthful, gentle, harmonious, and meaningful.

Wrong speech is a major cause of suffering. A husband tells a lie to his wife and sows the seeds of distrust in his family. Harsh, unloving speech leads to the breakup of relationships and marriages every day. A massive amount of the disputes we face in family life find their root in dishonesty, miscommunication, or a lack of communication at all. Certainly, right speech is indispensable if we hope to deal with others in constructive, enriching ways. Our loving words can guide our actions as we continue to tread the path.

IV

Right Action
(Sammā Kammanta)

Right action is, at its heart, a vow to protect the all beings, including oneself. Although this seems like a daunting task, we can start simply through the practice of the five precepts. These five vows are considered the minimum standard for the development of a virtuous life and the assurance of happiness for all beings who undertake them. In this world of immorality and self-destructive desire, the precepts provide protective armor for ourselves, as well as our families, our society, and the entire world in which we live. To act with right action is to gear all the things we do in our daily lives towards preserving and protecting the life and property of others, respecting the commitments we've made to others, and maintaining a sound mind free of obstruction. The precepts are the foundation of spiritual development and all people should observe them. They are as follows:

- I undertake the vow to refrain from destroying living creatures. This vow helps us cultivate love, compassion, and respect for life by avoiding its destruction.

- I undertake the vow to refrain from taking what is not given. This vow helps us cultivate generosity and contentment in life by avoiding stealing.

- I undertake the vow to refrain from sexual misconduct. This vow helps us cultivate love for our partners by avoiding unfaithfulness.

- I undertake the vow to refrain from false speech. This vow helps us cultivate truthfulness and honesty by avoiding the lies that so often harm the relationships we cherish.

- I undertake the vow to refrain from taking intoxicating drinks and drugs that lead to heedlessness. This vow helps us cultivate sobriety, control, and mindfulness by avoiding the things that can steer us from our path so easily.

The vow to refrain from drinking or drug use is especially important in our practice. An old Buddhist story illustrates the dangers of breaking even one precept:

> *"Once there was a layman who received the five precepts. At first, these precepts were very important to him and he kept them strictly. After a time, however, his past habits came back and longed for the taste of alcohol. He thought, "Of the five precepts, the one against drinking is really unnecessary. What's wrong with a sip or two?" So he bought three bottles of wine and started to drink. As he was drinking the second bottle, the neighbor's chicken ran into his house. "They've sent me a snack," he said. "I'll put this chicken on the menu to help keep down my wine." He then grabbed the bird and killed it, breaking the precept against killing as well as stealing. Suddenly, a woman stepped from the house next door, walked past and asked, "Say, have you seen my chicken?"*[xix]
>
> *Drunk as he was, and full of chicken, he slurred, "No, I didn't see no chicken. Your old chicken didn't run over here." So saying, he broke the precept against lying. As he sat on the ground, he looked at the woman and thought she was quite pretty. In the haze of his drunkenness, he advanced upon her and broke the precept against sexual misconduct. Soon misery followed him as he was*

> *punished for his crimes. He could not see that breaking one precept he thought was unimportant had led him to break all the precepts in the end. Never underestimate the value of keeping one precept; too often, all will be broken as soon as one is."*

When we live moral lives, we can cultivate wholesome states of mind that lead to spiritual growth and development. But if our mind is confused by violence, theft, sexual misconduct, dishonesty or intoxication, our attempts to do these things will fail. Maintaining the five basic precepts can greatly enrich one's life and bring about generosity, loving-kindness, compassion, and wisdom. The Buddha considered the five precepts as five great gifts that bestowed fearlessness, security and freedom to all beings. These vows are not burdens or restrictions but wonderful offerings we give to ourselves! We should delight as the trinity of right thought, speech, and action comes together; as these three wholesome practices join, we can use the insight gained to shape the way we earn our living.

V

Right Livelihood

(Sammā Ājīva)

Right livelihood mainly refers to the skillful ways we can earn our living. Holding down a constructive and balanced occupation – one of simplicity, self-sufficiency, and sustainability – is an excellent recipe for happiness and peace in our daily lives. The Buddha gave sound guidelines for lay people on how to earn their living; to protect ourselves as well as those around us in this world, we must avoid making our money from these five destructive livelihoods: dealing in the slave trade or with abused workers in foreign countries; dealing in poisons; dealing in the killing of animals for meat; dealing in intoxicants like alcohol and illegal drugs; and dealing in weapons. If we are serious about developing moral behavior and purifying our minds, we cannot have these careers putting money in our wallets. By refusing to deal in suffering or exploitation, we can focus on beneficial livelihoods that generate compassion in ourselves and bring about positive changes in others.

The practice of right speech, right action, and right livelihood is collectively known as morality. By speaking kindly, acting compassionately, and living righteously, we can create relationships based on fairness, equality, and respect – respect for ourselves, our families, our friends, our acquaintances, and eventually the whole of humanity. By generating such nourishing and joyful interactions in our daily lives, the practice of morality helps to eliminate the remorse, confusion, and unwholesomeness that cloud our thoughts. And when our mind is no longer buffeted back and forth by such destructive behaviors, we can begin the development of concentration in the following step.

VI

Right Effort

(Sammā Vāyāma)

Right effort is the hard work required to cross the ocean of suffering to the shores of liberation. No matter how intellectually solid or ethically sound we are, if we don't put effort into moving forward, we will end up backsliding or at the very least thrashing about, unable to follow our practice to its logical conclusion. Right effort energizes our minds, making it ready for further development. When we exert ourselves in the pursuit of meditation and mental purity, we emerge invigorated, efficient, and always ready to keep pushing forwards towards freedom. This practice will not succeed without some sweat! Luckily, to guide us, the Buddha laid out four kinds of right effort towards which we can strive.

First, we must exercise effort to prevent. This is the energy we expend to thwart the unwholesome states that attempt to find footholds in our minds. We pledge to restrain, control and guard our six senses with mindfulness; if we do not, we can't help but fall prey to the ambush of greed, hatred and delusion that waits for us to put our guard down.

As any doctor would tell you, prevention is better than a cure. However, we simply can't stop every single unskillful thought from finding its way into our thought process. If this happens, we shouldn't beat ourselves up. Instead, we simply need to be vigilant and overcome these unwholesome states so our mental calm can be restored. This is the effort to overcome –the energy we expend to remove any unwholesome states of mind that we discover inside ourselves. We endeavor to remove these negative feelings with a firm but gentle hand.

This pattern of destructive or simply useless thoughts arising day in and day out is certainly one most of us are familiar with. Sometimes our minds seem driven crazy with endless unproductive thoughts. These distractions draw a lot of energy from us; you could call it Compulsive Obsessive Thinking Syndrome. But luckily, there are tools the Buddha gave us to remain in control. We must think positively and selectively instead of letting a cascade of unhealthy thoughts overwhelm us. I use the term Thought Management Techniques (TMT) for the Buddha's five ways of overcoming these unintended, unwholesome thoughts:[x]

•**Replacement method:** First, we can make an effort to replace unwholesome states of mind with wholesome states of mind. For instance, we can replace thoughts of greed with thoughts of non-greed (generosity), thoughts of hatred or anger with thoughts of non-hatred (loving-kindness), and thoughts of cruelty with thoughts of non-cruelty (compassion). By combating these harmful thoughts with their opposites, we can go a long way towards banishing them from our minds. However, if unskillful thoughts still arise, then try the second technique.

- **Reflection method:** We can reflect on the fact that evil states of mind lead to unhappiness while skillful states of mind lead to joy. We can envision the negative results of our greed and anger and couple those with the positive effects of our compassion and generosity.

- **Redirection method:** Whenever disturbing thoughts arise, redirecting our mind to something else can help to dispel them. We can temporarily abandon the present meditation object and direct our mind to a wholesome, inspiring object, such as the Buddha, Dhamma, or Sangha. Even simply focusing on our breath can help to chase away anger and frustration. Once anger subsides, we can then return to our main focus.

- **Retracing method:** In this approach, we trace back the causes and conditions that lead to the arising of the disturbing thoughts. For instance, when fear arises, try to trace it to its origin – aversion to the present danger. This aversion is due to craving, affection, and attachment we have for a situation we aren't currently in. According to the Buddha, "From affection springs grief, from affection springs fear. For one who is wholly free from affection there is no grief, whence then fear?"[xi] We might ask ourselves where lust comes from and trace it back to our same attachment and ignorance. If we feel anger towards a child, husband, or wife, we can try to retrace the reason for our anger back to our desire and attachment, our need to have things go "right." By retracing a particular thought from its origin, we can unearth the true cause and weaken or eradicate its result.

• **Resolution method:** Here, we make a strong determination to get rid of the distracting thoughts. We should use every ounce of our effort to overcome them, refusing to let them control us. John Forsyth recommends that you avoid buying into your thoughts[xii] without examination; The Buddha advised us to "use the mind to crash the mind." This can be accomplished by directly applying awareness and mindfulness to that specific negative mind state. Mentally noting difficult mind states can be very useful in confronting the issue at hand and eventually banishing the negative thought for good – and when our mind is free from distracting thoughts, we can experience greater happiness as we continue to tread the path to final freedom.

We must remember that cleansing the mind of negative thoughts is only half the picture. The second effort, the effort to develop, is the energy we spend to cultivate the wholesome states of mind that we have inside us. When thoughts of generosity, loving-kindness, compassion arise, we can try to refine and develop them so that our expressions of these qualities become more natural and polished. As each positive thought comes into being, we hold it close and nurture it until it reaches its full potential.

Similarly, we must exert effort to keep hold of these wholesome states of mind. This is the effort to maintain. When perfect, wholesome states of mind have already arisen, we try our best to make sure they don't end up just fleeting glimpses but sustained, solid thoughts that can stay with us for long periods of time. So whenever thoughts of loving kindness or compassion arise, we try to maintain them, not allowing opposite states such as anger or hatred to take their place.

Determination

Determination (Adhitthāna in Pāli) is the fuel that keeps our practice moving. Without willpower and resolution, spiritual growth and development never leave the station! Through determination, we can keep the negative thoughts at bay and strive on towards our goal of freedom from suffering. Our daily practice might begin by promising ourselves that we will maintain the five basic precepts throughout our lives. The maintaining of these precepts is the key to success; with them, the gates leading to all wholesome states of mind open themselves. Can you imagine what would happen if, for just one day, the whole world made the effort to preserve life and not break the first precept? The whole of human history would never be the same!

Maintaining mindfulness in our daily activities is another practice that takes determination. We can make our meditation practice our vacuuming, eating, walking, or speaking; with effort, any of the millions of little activities that make up our day can become our daily practice. This mindfulness may not be as intense as our daily formal meditation, but being determined even in relaxed, moment-to-moment attention can make a huge difference. Please be clear, our determination should be practical and realistic. Some people decide after a retreat that they are lazy if they don't meditate for two or three hours a day. But soon they're exhausted; in just a week or two, their daily practice is nothing more than patting the Buddha statue as they head out the door. Don't let this happen! Be humble and set up a realistic approach for yourself. Determination is about endurance and dedication, not superhuman promises that we can't possibly fulfill.

Up until our final liberation, we must be diligent in promoting these constructive and wholesome mind states with hard work and energy.

VII

Right Mindfulness

(Sammā sati)

"Mindfulness" in English simply means to remember or to recollect. However, *Sati* as taught by the Buddha has a more specific meaning: to be aware, in the present moment, of everything going on within us and around us. Mindfulness is like a mirror, showing our experience to us without adding or subtracting anything. Without mindfulness, thoughts quickly become impulsive and habitual, leading to harmful words and actions and then later to regret; but with mindfulness, we can overcome and control our sensations, thoughts, and emotions. We can be aware of greed, anger or delusion, even when they are only in their subtlest forms. By allowing us to objectively see, with bare attention, the many different experiences we are having at any given moment, mindfulness can lead us to recognize the true nature of our experience and guide us on the path towards liberation.

VIII

Right Concentration
(Sammā Samādhi)

In this context, right concentration refers to the four meditative absorptions, which we call *jhāna*. *Jhāna* is achieved through the attainment of full concentration. During the jhānas, there is a complete but temporary suspension of the five hindrances that can prevent progress in our meditation: sensual desire, anger, sleepiness and dullness, restlessness and worry, and doubt or uncertainty. Although this concentration is helpful, it is not a way to permanent freedom – but when coupled with insight, these states can facilitate incredible spiritual advancement.

The trio of right effort, right mindfulness and right concentration forms the group we refer to as concentration. Each facet plays an important role in guiding our meditation practice - right effort keeps unskillful mental states at bay while allowing skillful mental states to arise; right mindfulness utilizes this effort to keep us alert and on guard; and right concentration brings the products of our mindful effort together in a single, unified state. As a result, our mind will be workable for even deeper insight meditation.

Although right concentration is the eighth factor in the Noble Eightfold Path, it is by no means the least important. The Buddha told us that concentrated mind see things as they really are; with such a mind, we can clearly observe the four Noble truths objectively in every single moment of our lives. This allows us to return full-circle to the first section of the path, wisdom, and realize completely and directly what we started off only knowing intellectually. In this way, our path is truly complete. Only joy, peace, and freedom from suffering will follow.

Meditation and the Noble Eightfold Path

Exploring and understanding the Noble Eightfold Path is an extensive but rewarding undertaking. Here is a quick summary of the benefits of meditation, according to the Noble Eightfold Path:

Right understanding allows us to know the true nature of our existence and embrace all aspects of life, even the difficult experiences of sickness, ageing, and death. By seeing our reality as it truly is, we can call upon a newfound security and peace, free from delusion and fear.

Right thought allows us to be more generous, contented, and kind, leading not only to greater personal happiness but also improved relationships with those we love.

Right speech allows us to deal openly and honestly with others, even in difficult situations. We can delight in forging trusting bonds with those we love and never fear the repercussions of deceit.

Right action allows us to offer the gifts of freedom, safety, and fearlessness to all creatures throughout the world. By following the precepts, we can live purely and above reproach, embodying kindness and respect for everyone we interact with.

Right livelihood allows us to support ourselves through beneficial and rewarding careers, enriching the world around us while helping maintain dignity and self-reliance.

Right effort allows us to let go of unskillful mind states while nurturing skillful ones. When combined with mindfulness, we can protect ourselves from the influence of negative thoughts and feelings while developing strong, untainted minds for ourselves.

Right mindfulness has many benefits; according to the Buddha, right mindfulness is the direct path to purification. We lose our greed, hatred, and delusion in favor of non-attachment compassion, and wisdom. This seems like plenty on its own, but mindfulness brings with it four other benefits as well: the overcoming of sorrow and lamentation, the disappearance of grief and pain, attainment of the true way, and the realization of Nibbāna. Mindfulness offers a solution for not only weathering life's hardest moments but also for allowing us to fully understand the root causes of suffering. You could say that one mindful thought a day keeps the *dukkha* away!

DHAMMA CAKKA
WHEEL OF DHAMMA
Noble Eightfold Path

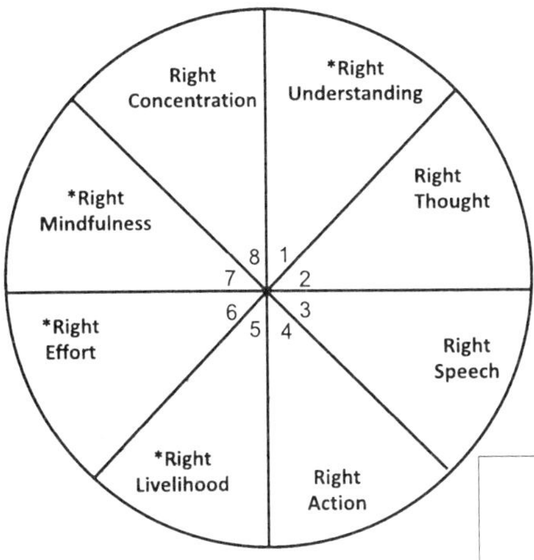

Noble Eightfold Path

Morality ↓	3 Right Speech 4 Right Action 5 Right Livelihood
Concentration ↓	6 Right Effort 7 Right Mindfulness 8 Right Concentration
Wisdom	*1 Right Understanding 2 Right Thought

* = Three Cardinal Factors

Figure 1: The relationship between the eight factors of the Eightfold Noble Path and the three groups of training known as Morality (Sīla), Concentration (Samādhi) and Wisdom (Pañña)

Practicing Formal Mindfulness Meditation

You can spend years in the classroom learning how to drive a car, but unless you actually get behind the wheel and start driving, you'll never be able to get to your destination safely. In the same way, it's all well and good to know intellectually the eight components of our spiritual path. However, in order to realize them on a deep, direct level, we must turn to formal meditation. The daily practice of meditation is the single most important tool we have for actually performing the *bhāvanā* we have until now simply talked about.

This practice is known specifically as insight meditation or *vipassanā*: In Pāli, *vi* means a special way and *passanā* means to see, observe, discern or contemplate. Together, *vipassanā* meditation is understanding experience in a special way through meditation. Vipassanā means to see things as they really are, by seeing that they are impermanent, unsatisfactory, and without essential self. The object of insight meditation is to realize an ultimate reality rather than taking just a quick glance at a conceptual reality.

Outwardly, this is simple enough. Just take a seat on a cushion or chair. Cross your legs any way that you find comfortable while keeping your body straight but not rigid. Take a moment to direct attention to your body; be aware of any areas of tension, tightness or stiffness, and try to relax them gently. Close (or half-close) your eyes and rest your hands in your lap with one hand on the other. Once you have found a position that is relaxed but steady, please take a few slow, deep breaths.

Focus your attention on the area of the body where you feel the breath most clearly. For most this is either the abdomen, right above the belly button, or at the tip of the nostrils. Find a place where you can feel distinctly the in and out or rising and falling of the breath. Be mindful of this breathing in and out; move your mind, so to speak, down to the abdomen or nose until you feel fully in touch with the sensations there. Let the breath be as natural as possible. There is no need to control anything. We are just being aware of what is happening naturally. We must mentally note these things in the present moment, not thinking about the past or future.

Make a mindful effort to understand the nature of breath. Note the warmth or coolness you may feel as you inhale, or the slight pressure you may feel as your abdomen rises. Try and pay attention to the full range of sensations felt at the point of observation you have chosen. Please remember that we are simply trying to be mindful, trying to understand the reality of our experience. We are not trying to make the breath longer or shorter. We are not trying to create any thoughts or concepts. We are just being aware of the breath in that moment.

As we settle into this rhythm, we can begin to apply the three kinds of full understanding laid out in the ancient Buddhist commentaries, namely:

- **Full understanding by knowing:** Know what you're looking for, in this case the breath, and be clear on what comprises it.

- **Full understanding by investigation:** Look at this phenomenon through the lens of the three marks of existence – impermanence, dissatisfaction, and selflessness – and come to see it as it truly is.

- **Full understanding by abandoning:** Let go of false views such as "This is my breath" or "I am breathing" in order to completely grasp the true nature of the breath without conceptualizing or labeling.

Should another sensation, such as pain or discomfort or cold arise, treat it as you did your breath. Simply guide your mindful attention towards the spot where the sensation is occurring and attempt to understand what you are feeling with full understanding; know that the sensation exists, examine its impermanence, its dissatisfying nature, and its selflessness, and finally abandon all the wrong views that accompany it. In this way, we can slowly learn to see all experience objectively and without attachment or aversion. This is the way to freedom from suffering.

As we focus on the breath mindfully, emotions, thoughts, and feelings will inevitably arise in those who are not very advanced. If this happens, don't beat yourself up! Even seasoned meditators must deal with such wayward thoughts. Just treat them as you would treat any other arising sensation. Know them, examine them, and abandon the destructive false notions you may have about them. In the beginning, you might have trouble dealing with difficult emotions; if so, The Mindfulness-Based Stress Reduction workbook[xiii] lays out the acronym RAIN to help:

- **R stands for recognize:** We must first mindfully be aware of the arising thought.

- **A stands for acknowledge:** Do not try and repress or stamp out the thought. Instead, simply be honest and state to yourself "thinking, thinking" quietly in your head.

- **I stands for investigate:** Simply examine the thought mindfully and realize its impermanence.

- **N stands for Non-identify:** We must never say "I am sad" or "I am thinking too much." Do not make your thoughts into who you are. Realize that like a pain in your back or a breeze on your face, they are simply arising and ceasing. You are not an angry person; anger has simply arisen.

By observing all things objectively with the three kinds of understanding, we will begin to fully realize the true nature of our experience – impermanence, dissatisfaction, and selflessness – and come to see for ourselves the Four Noble Truths. Even in a simple breath, we can feel discomfort, become restless, or fall into frustration. This is the First Noble Truth, the simple statement that we suffer.

Mindfully, we can ask ourselves why the suffering arises. We can examine the root of the frustration and see that it is based in our desire to be flawless; we can trace our restlessness back to our desire for constant stimulation; we can even trace our discomfort back to our aversion from pain. This is the Second Noble Truth, the statement that our attachment to what we desire leads us to suffer. Between breaths, as our concentration grows and our defilements fade away, we can temporarily taste the freedom that comes from the cleansing of the mind. We realize directly that we are peaceful, happy, and free from suffering when we cling to nothing. This is the Third Noble Truth, the statement that abandoning our craving can lead to ultimate liberation from suffering. The Fourth Noble Truth that of the Eightfold Path, can also be understood as we mindfully examine the positive and negative results of our actions. We can come to see that acting immorally, unwisely, and without proper concentration will lead us to more defilement while being compassionate, wise, and mindful will bring us joy and contentment. When we see this through meditation, we have realized the Fourth Noble Truth, the statement that right understanding, intention, speech, action, livelihood, effort, mindfulness, and concentration are the building blocks of the spiritual life.

As our practice develops, we begin to fully realize the true nature of our experience. Consequently, right concentration will organically develop.

Turning Obstacles into Opportunities

During my first winter at the Bhāvanā Society, we had plenty of snow. I was assigned to a kuti, a small room for monks that had no water or electricity. Because we had to heat our kuti with wood, it used to be very dry inside. One monk advised me to keep a container filled with water around to reduce the humidity. Although this seemed like a great solution, soon I realized that it meant carrying a heavy jar of water every day from the main building and back. For the first couple weeks, I struggled back and forth daily. Once, it snowed hard and I had to shovel and shovel just to create a small path to my room. Eventually a blizzard struck and the snow was knee-deep. I used to push through step by step, carrying water all the while. It was hard work!

I did this for a few weeks until I realized a solution. Instead of shoveling snow aside, I decided to collect it in the big container and put it on the wood stove. Soon I had more water than I would ever need to keep my hut from drying out.

Even after we decide to set forth on the Noble Eightfold Path, we will still come across roadblocks like this. Although most of us don't wake up to a doorway blocked with snow, no one can dedicate themselves to meditation practice without occasionally hitting these rough patches. The Buddha himself identified these as the five hindrances. They aren't physical things like sickness or pain. Instead, these five hindrances are mental afflictions that throw us off the path towards true happiness and enlightenment. These five are sensual desire, ill will, sloth and torpor, restlessness and worry, and doubt.

Anyone who has spent even a few minutes in meditation knows these five hurdles, and just as I first pushed myself to the point of exhaustion simply to plow through them, too often we as meditators adopt a "grin-and-bear-it" attitude that only results in frustration and fatigue. Luckily, the Buddha taught us a way to simply transform these unfortunate situations from hindrances to solutions.

Sensual desires

Sensual desires are the cravings we have for the five strands of sense pleasure, or in other words, for pleasant forms, sounds, smells, tastes, tactile sensations and thoughts or ideas. Some desires may be subtle while others may grip you intensely. Either way, remember that they are just emotions and observe them accordingly. We all like to taste good food, listen to nice music, look at beautiful things, and dream up big ideas about people and places and so on and so on. These things aren't evil or perverse; there is no problem with the sense objects *per se.* However, our *attachment* to these things can delay the progress of our mental cultivation. There's nothing wrong with looking out your window on a scenic drive, but if you stop every twenty yards to soak up the scenes, you'll never reach your destination!

The way we work with desires is to be mindful of desire itself. Earlier, we discussed the three marks of existence –

impermanence, unsatisfactoriness, and selflessness. It turns out that our desire bears those same three marks as well! We may not be able to just banish our attachment immediately, but we can come to realize that like all things, it will pass.

When you find yourself wanting a nice big slice of cake, be mindful of the feelings that cause your mouth to water. When you find yourself lusting, be mindful of the feelings that cause you to heat up inside. Do the same for everything. Too often we think that meditation should be an easy, fun activity; we find ourselves disheartened and think we're practicing wrong. But don't be shaken! The greatest breakthroughs in meditation come from examining these rough spots and seeing their true nature instead of just being sidetracked into the side streets of selfish desire.

Ill will

Whenever someone or something stops us from realizing our desires, there arises a sense of frustration. We develop aversion and distaste for anything that separates us from what we want. Anything that turns our desire on its head is liable to bring up resentment and bitterness. When we find ourselves caught up in traffic jam while rushing to an appointment, when we spill something on our favorite piece of clothing, when anything keeps us from getting what we want, when we want, this resentment begins to arise. Being filled with anger is like holding your gas pedal to the floor and speeding down the highway; you'll find that you're moving far too quickly to judge your next move, and before you know it you've crashed!

Like desire, these feelings can differ in intensity, from mild annoyance to overpowering hatred. Sadly, the original problem, whether it be a dent in our new car or wayward thoughts in our meditation, is responsible only for a small portion of the anger. The rest comes from the way we handle that situation. We try to justify our anger and begin to indulge it; we feed the flames with unguarded thoughts instead of extinguishing them with mindfulness.

We can think of our minds like a pack of matches. The surface of the matchbox has the potential to bring about a flame, just as the matchstick has the potential to give rise to a flame once struck. Both factors contribute to creation of the flame. In the same way, the person who makes us angry may be the matchstick striking us, but unless we have the potential for anger and hatred inside us, we won't make a flame. You can't bring about a flame by striking a match on a piece of cloth! Next time someone brings up anger inside you, take a moment to be thankful that they've revealed a spot on your mind where a match can be struck.

If we don't acknowledge the many roots of our anger, we can become bitter and resentful, seeking revenge and inflicting hurt. How many violent acts occur every day because people cannot see that they have a hand in their anger? Every day, we can see the terrible results of those who forget the Buddha's words: "The only thing worth killing is our anger."

We must deal with anger as it is – inside of us and only arising with our consent. We cannot stamp out anger out with physical things or with more anger. We must cut it off in the mind itself. Contemplate what brings about anger and be mindful of the ill will itself, not the object it is directed towards. Pay attention on the effect of anger on the body and mind. When we can come to see the emotion in our mind objectively without getting caught up in it, we can strip it of any power it may have. After it is weakened with mindfulness and loving-kindness, a strong dose of wisdom can do wonders for purging it completely.

Restlessness and worry

Restlessness is any excitement, agitation or disquiet in the mind, whereas worry is any sense of remorse we have over the evil things we've done or the good things we've neglected to do. Both distract the mind, driving it off-track like a car taking a wrong turn while the driver is busy texting or listening to music.Not only does the driver take longer to get to their destination, but the wear down the tires quite a bit! In the same way, we only exhaust ourselves when we follow the negative tangents that arise when we give into restlessness and worry.

As always, the way to overcome restlessness is to be mindful of restlessness itself. Like all other hindrances, make restlessness the object of your meditation. If you still have trouble calming yourself, you might want to turn your attention to the physical body instead of the mind for a moment. Be mindful of your sitting posture or the sensation of the body touching the cushion. Once restlessness has subsided, you may go back to your primary object, the breath. If restlessness persists still, attempt to focus on the wonderful compassion and wisdom of the Buddha, the beauty of the Dhamma (the teaching), and the dedication of the Sangha (the noble Buddhist community). Reflections on these three things, known as the three jewels, can arouse gladness, joy, tranquility, happiness, and concentration. Remember to return to your primary focus, the breath, once restlessness disappears.

Sloth and torpor

Sometimes we might feel heaviness in the body or fogginess in the mind. Much like driving in the fog, we can't see things as they pass by us, even while others can see us just fine. Many refuse to meditate if they feel anything like this, afraid that they will have no progress. But no one stops driving just because there is fog on the road! We just need to be especially mindful and soon we find we can clear the fog ourselves.

Sloth and torpor (or sleepiness and dullness) may arise for different reasons. It is very important to identify the cause of your sleepiness. This will help you to skillfully address the problem. If you find yourself sleepy after a large meal, it might help to take a brisk walk or to do your meditation before eating. Otherwise, if you find your fogginess is coming from daily fatigue, just try being mindful of your body. If that does not work, make sure to get a little rest. Without proper sleep and relaxation, any activity, especially meditation, can be a challenge.

As for the sluggishness that has no physical cause, but just comes for a tired mind, again mindfulness is the solution. Sometimes, without a proper object to investigate, the mind can grow bored and begin to shut down. Make sure you keep it active with a healthy dose of concentration. Otherwise, try mindfulness meditation in different postures, or opt for walking or standing meditation instead.

A few years ago, I went to Burma to learn meditation. During the two months of silent meditation, I saw a Chinese monk who was hit with intense sleepiness. He nodded off constantly! Halfway through the retreat, he solved his problem by sitting right in front of a large pillar in the meditation hall. Each time he began to nod off, he would catch himself just before he hit the hard concrete. He never once bruised his forehead! While this is a bit extreme, we have to remember to be creative; although a foggy mind can really derail your practice, it's not hard to find your own way to shake away the clouds!

Doubt

Even with a mind clouded by anger or tiredness, we can still find our destination eventually – but if we stop at a fork in the road and refuse to take either direction, we'll never make it at all! Uncertainty and doubt in regard to our practice, training, or instruction can throw us off track fastest of all.

Doubt is difficult to cure because its root is delusion. At its heart, doubt arises when we cannot discern between what is skillful and unskillful, blameworthy and not blameworthy, or wholesome and unwholesome. For example, during meditation, we may start to wonder if mindfulness can really help us to overcome our problems. We stop watching the breath and get lost in a million little questions: Should I practice meditation or not? Is Buddhism for me or not? Is this person a good teacher or not? This is not a healthy skepticism, but instead a second-guessing that helps no one, least of all ourselves. We may even begin to doubt our ability to practice meditation or our ability to be truly happy. This self-doubt is the worst of all.

During my early meditation practice in India, I had doubts about which tradition to follow in my life. I investigated many philosophies but most of the time I felt dissatisfied. I had been born a Roman Catholic and pursued more of that in India by going to church where the Mass was conducted in Hindi. Of course I did not understand Hindi, but I had confidence that God had "seen me" attending the Sunday service. Sadly, I felt hollow soon after. I tried another route and was confirmed in the Baha'i Faith in New Delhi. I practised a little bit of Hinduism, following a form of yoga known as Raja yoga. I read books on Sufism and visited their temple; Tibetan Buddhism followed after. Sometimes I was confused regarding the truth and the best way to lead my life spiritually. I could take the bite off this confusion by calling myself a general practitioner of spirituality or a student of life, but finally I decided to follow Theravada Buddhism and I have been very sure of my path ever since.

Many people know exactly how I felt. It is not uncommon nowadays for a person to pursue a variety of philosophies. On Monday, they might go to a Sufi dance. On Tuesday, time for African shamanism. On Wednesday, Tibetan Tonglen, and on Thursday it's Hindu Satsang or Darshan.

Native American ascending is the place to be on Friday with a follow-up of Buddhist vipassanā meditation on Saturday. Don't forget Mass on Sunday! I'm sure a lot of you know exactly how I felt.

So many people today will reply, when asked about their practice, "I follow many spiritual paths but I do not want to commit to any one religion. I don't like any labels." I felt this way once too. However, we must admit that pursuing a different tradition every day in hopes to reach a deep state of spiritual enlightenment is like digging many small holes to reach a treasure buried deep underground. You have many entry points but none go deep enough to pay off in the end. This cycle of searching, finding, and abandoning is fueled by the same self-doubt that can derail a practitioner even when they've found a path and begun to dig deep.

The only cure for this vicious cycle is confident faith – not blind faith, but an assuredness based on understanding and wisdom. To develop this trust and confidence in the Buddha's teachings, we must pay close attention to discern what is skillful and unskillful, what is helpful and unhelpful, and what is true and untrue. We can't be led like sheep, unquestioning and gullible, but we can't get caught up in second-guessing and needlessly criticizing either. The wonderful thing about the Noble Eightfold Path is that it was not revealed by a higher power or sent down to a special few - it's available to all of us if we look deep enough into our own hearts! We can see these truths directly with our own minds and realize their benefits in the here and now. If we question, investigate, and study, we can come to a full and rich faith that guides us as we move on our path of self-discovery.

Living your Understanding

I'd like to close with a sacred Hindu tale. It talks about the ancient days, before our time, when all men and women were said to be Gods. After seeing them misuse their divinity, Brahma, the highest God, decided to take it away and hide it, never to be found again. But Brahma could not find a suitable place. Some of the other lesser Gods gathered and counseled, "Brahma, let us bury the divinity of man deep inside the Earth." But Brahma answered, "No, man will one day dig deep and discover this divinity again." The Gods then thought and came up with a new plan. "Let us sink the Divinity into the deepest oceans of the Earth." But Brahma shook his head and responded, "No, for sooner or later, mankind will dive into the deepest places in all the oceans and discover this divinity again."

The Gods debated for many hours but still came out perplexed. "There is no place on this world to hide their divinity," they cried in exasperation. "Man will climb the mountains! Man will dig into the ground! Man will dive deep into the oceans! There is no place where their curiosity will not take them!" But Brahma smiled. "This is what we'll do," he said. "We will hide it in the deepest part of man himself. This is the only place where man will never look."

Since then, the Hindu tale tells us, humankind has crisscrossed the Earth, diving, digging, climbing, exploring, searching everywhere for something that can only be found deep in themselves."[xiv]

So ask yourself, what are you searching for? Have you set out across the seas and dug deep into the earth? Have you chased desires and run from fears, each time hoping that they will guide you to the place where your ultimate goal is hidden? And ask yourself, have you ever found it? Or do you still suffer, running to and fro in the hopes that one day you will stumble upon the treasure map that will reveal the way to peace, happiness and freedom? You don't have to look! The Noble Eightfold Path is that map, that course that promises to lead you into liberation – a treasure that you won't find on the highest mountains or the deepest seas, but only right here, deep inside.

This universal passageway to the ultimate freedom is simple enough to be followed by any person who is willing to see the Dhamma through mindfulness, wisdom, concentration, and ethical living. Our potential to gain enlightenment is already inside us, waiting to be discovered in this very life. Greed, hatred, and delusion can be conquered; peace, joy, and freedom and be found. I know that if you are reading this now, then your ultimate treasure is right under your nose – in fact, it's only a breath away!

May all beings be well, happy and peaceful.

Appendix

The following are some simple daily reflections and meditations to help us develop and maintain confidence, determination, and joy during our practice:

Giving

"May I always be generous and open minded. May I give to others the threefold gifts in accordance with their need – joyfully with a heart free from the taint of selfishness, with a heart overflowing with kindness and compassion."

Ethical conduct

"May my actions of the body, speech and mind always accord with the precepts I have undertaken: Pure and clean, free from breach or blemish. May I always be noble, lofty and upright, a model for the entire world."

Renunciation

"May I not be selfish and self-possessive. May I be able to sacrifice my pleasure for the sake of others. May I always have the discernment and strength of will to renounce the worldly life and go forth into homelessness in order to lead the pure spiritual life. May I be able to relinquish all points of inner attachment in order to enter the exalted concentration and liberation of the mind."

Energy
"May I be filled with inexhaustible energy, vigor and fortitude in cultivating the path to enlightenment and working for the benefit of others."

Wisdom
"May my wisdom grow as vast as space, as deep as the ocean, and as luminous as the sun, dispelling the darkness of ignorance and illuminating the true nature of things."

Patience
"May I always be patient under all circumstances, no matter how difficult and challenging they might be. May I be forbearing and forgiving towards all beings, even towards those who revile, abuse, or harass me."

Truthfulness
"May I always speak the truth, live by the truth, and be devoted to truth in order to win the confidence of others."

Determination
"May I be fixed and unshakable in my determination to follow the way of the Buddha in life after life, without ever turning away due to laziness, fear, or doubt."

Loving-kindness
"May I develop a heart of boundless loving-kindness and great compassion–a heart vast, sublime, and immeasurable, embracing all beings."

Equanimity
"May I develop a mind of perfect equanimity, a mind that is just and impartial towards all beings, without bias or preferences; a mind that cannot be shaken by the four pairs of worldly winds (gain and loss, fame and defame, praise and blame, pleasure and pain)."

(Adapted from the article by Ven. Bhikkhu Bodhi)

Glossary of Pāli Terms

Anattā - The central doctrine of Buddhism. It means absence of an inherent or independent self. Other meaning includes lack of self-essence; "no-self"; impersonality; beyond control or no core. There is nothing within the bodily and mental phenomena, nor outside of them, can be found.

Anicca - Impermanence, the nature of all conditioned things; arising, passing and changing of things. It is the basic sign or mark of all conditioned phenomena. The characteristic of impermanence becomes apparent in its true nature by discerning "rising" and "falling."

Bhāvanā - Mental development or meditation. There are two main types: development of concentration and development of insight (wisdom).

Bhikkhu - Male fully ordained Buddhist monk under the Buddha dispensation. Up to the present day, a bhikkhu keeps 227 disciplinary rules, shaves his head, wears ochre-colored, orange, dark-brown or saffron robes, and lives dependent on alms food.

Bhante - An honorific title for a Buddhist monk in the Theravāda tradition. It means, "Venerable Sir".

Brahmā Vihāras–The four boundless states: loving-friendliness (loving- kindness), compassion, sympathetic or altruistic joy, and equanimity.

Dukkha - Suffering due attachment to impermanence things.

Dhamma - The teaching of Buddha; Fundamental truth.

dhamma - Any conditioned object or the unconditional; A phenomenon of nature; Constitution or nature of a thing.

Jhāna –Meditative absorptions. The quality of mind that is able to stick to an object and observe it without distractions.

Mettā –Loving-friendliness, loving-kindness or goodwill. The wish for all beings to enjoy internal and external safety; mental and physical happiness; and ease of well-being. One of the four divine abidings (Brahmā Vihāras)

Sati - Mindfulness -"observing power" of the mind that clearly and simply experiences an object without reacting to it.

Nibbāna– Unconditioned state. The deliverance from all kinds of suffering and misery such as: old age; disease; and death. It constitutes the highest and ultimate goal of all Buddhist aspirations.

Pāli – Language of the Theravāda Buddhist scriptures. It is thought to be the language spoken by the Buddha and his disciples.

Paññā– Intuitive knowledge of ultimate truth; understanding the four Noble Truth; Wisdom Group is one of the three kinds of trainings; Insight into the three characteristics of existence, impermanence, suffering, and non-self.

Samādhi – Concentration. It is one-pointedness of mind or fixing the mind on a single object.

Sila – Ethical conduct or morality. It is the first of the 3 kinds of training that form the three-fold division of the Noble Eightfold path i.e. morality, concentration, and wisdom.

Sutta – The discourse of the Buddha. They form the "Second Basket" of basic texts in Buddhism.

Vipassanā–The practice of observing or contemplating mental and physical processes in their aspect of impermanence, suffering, and selflessness nature.

Recommended Reading

- *Mindfulness in Plain English* by Bhante Gunaratana
- *Eight Mindfulness steps to Happiness* by Bhante Gunaratana
- *The Heart of Buddhist Meditation* by Nyanaponika Thera
- *The Four Foundations of Mindfulness*by Sayadaw U Silananda
- *The Treasure of Dhamma* by Ven. Sri K. Dhammananda
- *In This Very Life* by Sayadaw U Pandita
- *The Mind State called Beautiful* by Sayadaw U Pandita
- *Practical Insight Meditation* by Mahasi Sayadaw
- *Satipaṭṭhāna – The Direct path to Realization* by Venerable Anālayo
- *What the Buddha Taught* by Walpole Rahula
- *Awakening the Mind, Lightening the Heart* by His Holiness, The Dalai Lama

- *Insight Mediation* by Joseph Goldstein
- *The Experience of Insight* by Joseph Goldstein
- *A Path with Heart* by Jack Kornfield
- *Loving kindness* by Sharon Salzberg
- *Faith* by Sharon Salzberg

Address

The Uganda Buddhist Centre
Off- Entebbe Road, Garuga, Bulega, Entebbe
P.O. Box 898, Entebbe,
Uganda
East Africa.
URL: www.ugandabuddhistcenter.org

The Ugandan Buddhist Center is in the Theravada Buddhist tradition, but is open to other religious traditions as well.

The Ugandan Buddhist Center was founded by the Venerable Bhikkhu Buddharakkhita.

About the author

The Venerable Bhikkhu Buddharakkhita was born in Uganda, Africa. He first encountered Buddhism while living in India in 1990. In November, 2002, he received higher ordination under the late Venerable U Silananda at the Tathagata Meditation Center in California. He continued his meditation study and practice for eight years under the guidance of Bhante Gunaratana at the Bhāvanā Society in West Virginia. He is the founder and Abbot of the Uganda Buddhist Center in Uganda and has been teaching meditation in Australia, Asia, Europe, Brazil, and the United States. Besides spending time at the Uganda Buddhist Centre, he is a meditation instructor of Buddhist counseling psychology at the Sri Lanka International Buddhist Academy in Sri Lanka. He is a representative of Uganda to the World Buddhist Summit in Japan. He is also a spiritual adviser of Global Buddhist Relief, based in New Jersey, and the spiritual Adviser of Flowering Lotus Meditation Center in Magnolia, Mississippi. His book, *Planting Dhamma Seeds: The Emergence of Buddhism in Africa* tells the story of his religious and spiritual work in Africa.

End notes

[i]Bodhi, Bhikkhu., (2010), *The Noble Eightfold Path*, Kandy, Buddhist Publication Society, p. 50.

[ii]Majjhima Nikāya: *Saccavibhanga Sutta 141*: Bodhi, Bhikkhu; Ñanamoli, Bhikkhu., (2009), Boston; Wisdom Publication, p. 141.

[iii]Majjhima Nikāya: *Madhupindika Sutta 18* : Bodhi, Bhikkhu; Nanamoli, Bhikkhu. (2009), Boston; Wisdom Publication, p. 205.

[iv]Bodhi, Bhikkhu. *Nibbāna,* Viewed 3 May 2012, 2: 30 p.m<http://hkims.org/documents/Nibbana%20by%20 Bhikkhu%20 Bodhi.pdf>.

[v]Majjhima Nikāya: *Sammādiṭṭhi Sutta 9* : Bodhi, Bhikkhu; Nanamoli, Bhikkhu. (2009), Boston; Wisdom Publication, p. 205.

[vi]*The Dhammapada*, Verse 1, Buddharakkhita, Achariya., (2007) , Kandy; Buddhist Publication Society, p.3.

[vii]*The Dhammapada*, verse 2, Buddharakkhita, Achariya., (2007) , Kandy; Buddhist Publication Society, p. 4.

[viii]Gunaratana, Bhante., (2001) *Eight Mindfulness Step*, Boston, Wisdom Publication, p. 58.

[ix]*Buddhism: Key Stage 11* (2002), Yin, Jing,' Ho, W.Y., United Kingdom; Buddhist Education Foundation, p. 75.

[x]*Majjhima Nikāya: Vitakkasanthāna Sutta 20*: Bodhi, Bhikkhu; Ñanamoli, Bhikkhu. (2009), Boston; Wisdom Publications, p. 211.

[xi]*The Dhammapada*, Verse 213, Buddharakkhita, Achariya., (2007), Kandy; Buddhist Publication Society, p. 91-92.

[xii]Forsyth, John & Eifert, Georg, (2008), *The Mindfulness & Acceptance Workbook for Anxiety,* California; New Harbinger Publications, p. 193.

[xiii]Stahl, Bob & Goldstein, Elisha, (2009), *Mindfulness-Based Stress Reduction Work book,* California; New harbinger publications, p. 116.

[xiv]Butterworth, (2002), *An Old Hindu Legend about the Divinity of Mankind.* Viewed 3 May 2012, 3:00 pm <http://www.life-cycles-destiny.com/n1/anold.htm>

References

Primary Sources

A Translation of Majjhima Nikāya 20: Bodhi, Bhikkhu; Ñanamoli, Bhikkhu., (2009), Boston; Wisdom Publications.

A Translation of the Dīgha Nikāya, Walshe, Maurice., (1987, 1995), Boston, Wisdom Publications.

The Dhammapada, Verse 1, Buddharakkhita, Achariya., (2007), Kandy; Buddhist Publication Society.

Secondary Sources

Bodhi, Bhikkhu., (2010), The Noble Eightfold Path, Kandy, Buddhist Publication Society.

Gunaratana, Bhante., (2001), Eight Mindfulness Steps to Happiness, Boston, Wisdom Publications.

Stahl, Bob & Goldstein, Elisha., (2009), Mindfulness-Based Stress Reduction Work book, California; New harbinger publications.

Yin, Jing, Ho, W.Y., Buddhism: Key Stage 11, (2002), United Kingdom; Buddhist Education Foundation.